I didn't know that

mountains gush

lava

and

ash

an imprint of
The Millbrook Press
2 Old New Milford Road
Brookfield, Connecticut 06804

Concept, editorial, and design by
David West Children's Books
Designer: Flick Killerby
Illustrators: Ian Thompson, Peter Roberts – Allied Artists,
Jo Moore

Printed in Belgium

Library of Congress Cataloging-in-Publication Data
Oliver, Clare.
Mountains gush lava and ash: and other amazing facts
about volcanoes / by Clare Oliver ; illustrated by Ian Thompson.
p. cm. — (I didn't know that—)
Includes index.
Summary: Explores volcanoes on the ground, under the sea, and in
space, discussing their formation, eruptions, and lava and ash.
BN 0-7613-0820-2 (lib. bdg.). — ISBN 0-7613-0739-7 (trade hardcover)
1. Volcanoes—Juvenile literature. [1. Volcanoes.]
I. Thompson, Ian, 1964- ill. II. Title. III. Series.
QE521.3.O43 1998   98-18033
551.21—dc21   CIP AC

I didn't know that

mountains gush lava and ash

Clare Oliver

COPPER BEECH BOOKS
BROOKFIELD, CONNECTICUT

I didn't know that

the earth is covered in plates 7

the earth is full of holes 8

there are rivers of rock 10

mountains spit ash 13

ash can freeze people in time 14

waves can be 100 ft high 16

volcanoes make islands 19

there are chimneys under the sea 20

you can take a bath in mud 22

volcanoes fall asleep for centuries 24

there are volcanoes in space 26

volcanologists wear space suits 28

glossary 30

index 32

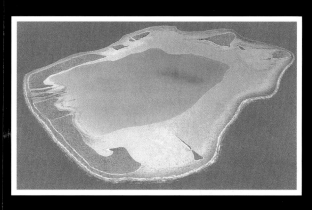

Introduction

Did *you* know that most volcanoes are under the sea? ... that volcanologists are volcano scientists? ... that the biggest volcano is on Mars?

Discover for yourself amazing facts about the earth's volcanoes and the people who study them. Learn about tsunamis, hot springs, black smokers, and about volcanoes of the past – and in space.

Watch for this symbol that means there is a fun project for you to try.

Is it true or is it false? Watch for this symbol and try to answer the question before reading on for the answer.

Don't forget to check the borders for extra amazing facts.

Copy the map of the earth below, or blow it up on a photocopier. Color it in, then cut along the fault lines. Can you fit all the *plates* back together? Can you find the Pacific Ocean plate? There are so many volcanoes around this plate that the area is called the Ring of Fire.

Most earthquakes are not even noticeable, but about every three years there is a violent one somewhere in the world. In 1970, an earthquake in Peru made roads crack and buildings collapse. It caused a massive landslide – and 66,000 deaths.

The San Andreas Fault in California is where two plates are sliding past each other in opposite directions. There have been lots of big earthquakes along this line. Even so, many people make their homes there.

I didn't know that

the earth is covered in plates. The earth's *crust* is made of pieces called plates. These don't join neatly – some overlap, and there are gaps between others. Volcanoes and earthquakes usually happen at *fault lines* where the edges of plates move apart or grate together.

The slow movement of fault lines is measured with a creepmeter!

I didn't know that

the earth is full of holes.

Volcanoes are openings in the earth's crust, often on a fault line. Rock below the earth's surface can get so hot it forms *magma*. When the pressure rises it blasts a hole and the hot melted rock, ash, and gas escape.

Geysers (above) are openings in the earth that shoot out fountains of boiling water. Volcanic heat boils water that is trapped underground.

Crater

Pipe

Dike

Cone

Volcanoes are named after Vulcan, Roman god of fire and metalworking.

True or false?
There is fire at the center of the earth.

Outer mantle (hot rock)

Outer core (liquid metal)

Inner core (solid metal)

Inner mantle (hot rock)

Answer: **False**
Long ago people believed that a fire inside our planet gave all volcanoes their fiery power. Now, we know the earth's core is metal and that a hot *mantle* of rock surrounds the core.

Vent

Magma chamber

When they erupt, volcanoes really blow their top! They leave a *crater*. If it is very big, it's called a *caldera*. The one above is on the Japanese volcano, Shirane. It's been so long since Shirane erupted that its crater has filled with rainwater and become a lake.

I didn't know that

there are rivers of rock.

When a volcano erupts, it squirts out hot, liquid rock called *lava*. Sometimes, the lava is slow and just oozes out. Sometimes, the lava is so runny it gushes in rivers, flowing at speeds up to 30 mph.

When a volcano shoots lava into the air it makes a fountain of fire that can reach 300 ft in height. Molten rock can also come out as house-sized lava bombs, little stones called lapilli, or clouds of ash and dust.

Pumice stone is hardened lava - it can help to soften your feet!

SEARCH & FIND FIND & SEARCH

Can you find five lava bombs?

True or false?
Lava has skin.

Answer: **True**

Pahoehoe (pa hoy hoy) is a very hot, fluid type of lava that grows a smooth skin on top as it cools. The hot flow continues underneath, even though the crust may be hard enough to walk across.

Warning – adult help needed!

Make an *eruption*! Half fill a jar with baking soda. Cut a circle out of cardboard. Make a slit to the middle and tape into a cone shape. Cut a hole at the top of the cone and place over the jar. Add some red food coloring to vinegar. Pour it into the jar, then stand back! This can be messy. Wear old clothes and do it outdoors!

True or false?
There really is a blue moon.

Answer: **True**
Floating clouds of volcanic ash do strange things to light. They can even make the moon and sun seem to glow blue or green!

The static in an ash cloud can also make lightning. To make static put a metal tray on a plastic bag. Attach a clay "handle" to the tray, then rub it around on the bag. Lift the tray and, with your other hand, touch its edge with a metal fork to see sparks fly!

Mount St. Helens is 4,500 years old - young for a volcano.

I didn't know that

mountains spit ash. The most violent volcanoes blast out ash and gas. The force of Mount St. Helens' eruption in 1980 was as powerful as 500 atomic bombs going off. The cloud gave amazing red sunsets and ash fell over 700 miles away in Colorado.

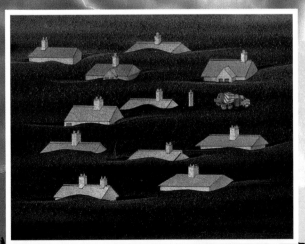

Ash clouds can block out the sun for days. In 1973, the cloud from an eruption on Heimaey (left), off Iceland, left behind a thick blanket of black ash. In some places the ash was over 19 ft deep.

13

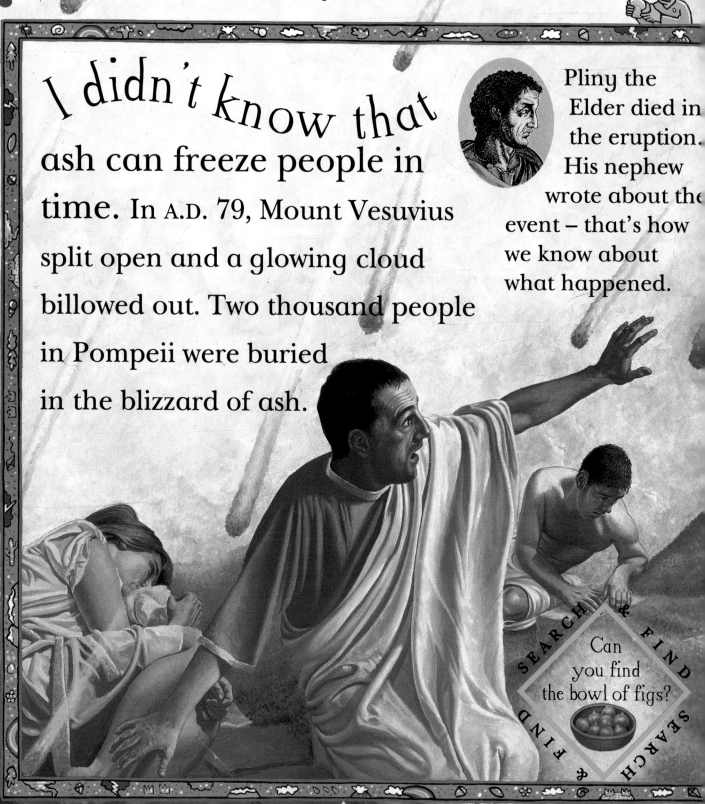

I didn't know that

ash can freeze people in time. In A.D. 79, Mount Vesuvius split open and a glowing cloud billowed out. Two thousand people in Pompeii were buried in the blizzard of ash.

Pliny the Elder died in the eruption. His nephew wrote about the event – that's how we know about what happened.

SEARCH & FIND
Can you find the bowl of figs?
FIND & SEARCH

Pompeii lay forgotten for 1,600 years. Another eruption uncovered the original town. The bodies had decayed leaving people-shaped holes in the hardened ash. By filling these molds with plaster of Paris, archaeologists made models of the Romans – and their pets!

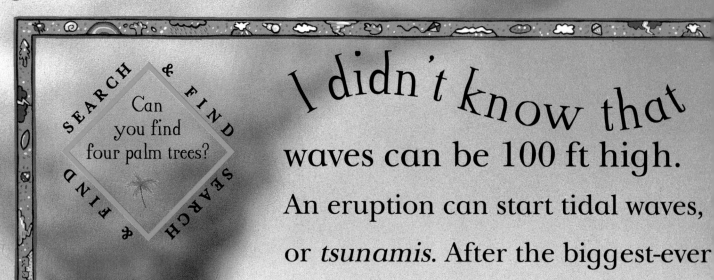

! Tsunamis are powerful enough to cross the Pacific Ocean.

SEARCH & FIND & FIND & SEARCH

Can you find four palm trees?

I didn't know that

waves can be 100 ft high.

An eruption can start tidal waves, or *tsunamis*. After the biggest-ever volcanic eruption, at Krakatoa, over 36,000 people were drowned in huge black walls of water.

True or false?
Tsunamis are always caused by volcanoes.

Answer: **False**
Tsunamis happen after earthquakes, too. Tsunamis following the Chilean earthquake in 1960 were so powerful that they toppled the statues on Easter Island.

The Berouw (above) was thrown 2 miles upriver by the Krakatoa tsunami in 1883. She is still there today

The artist Katsushika Hokusai painted a very famous picture of a tsunami. Called *The Great Wave*, it shows an enormous tsunami in front of the Japanese volcano Mount Fujiyama, which is actually 12,000 ft high.

Tsunami is Japanese for "wave breaking in the harbor."

SEARCH & FIND & SEARCH & FIND & SEARCH

Can you find three fulmars?

Iceland is a land of fire and ice, with several active volcanoes and geysers. It formed over millions of years from volcanic eruptions in the Mid-Oceanic Ridge. It is over 50,000 times bigger than Surtsey.

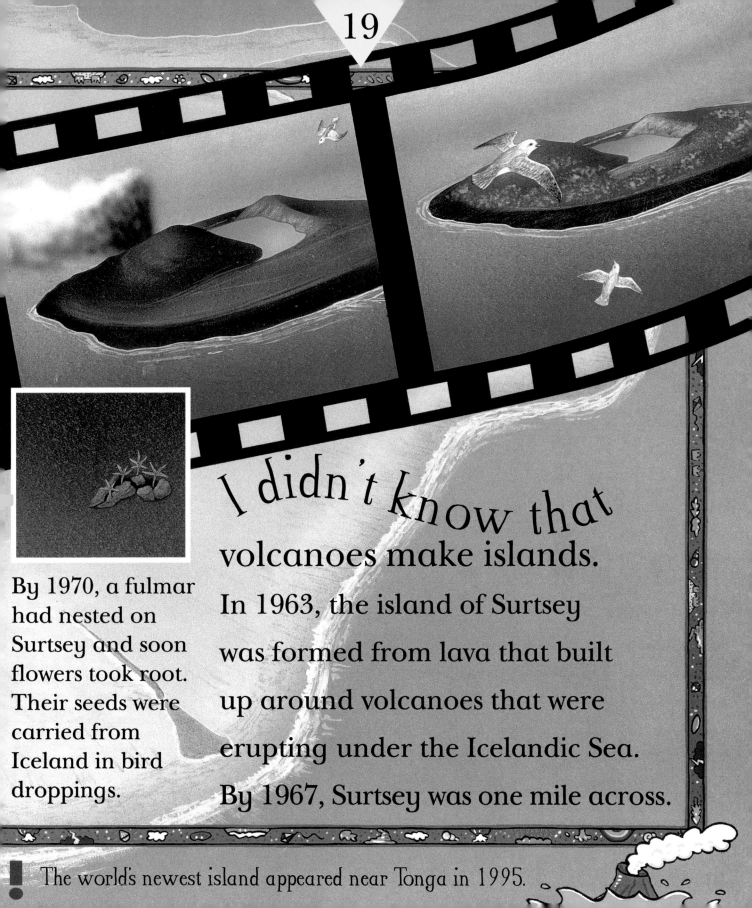

I didn't know that volcanoes make islands.

In 1963, the island of Surtsey was formed from lava that built up around volcanoes that were erupting under the Icelandic Sea. By 1967, Surtsey was one mile across.

By 1970, a fulmar had nested on Surtsey and soon flowers took root. Their seeds were carried from Iceland in bird droppings.

The world's newest island appeared near Tonga in 1995.

I didn't know that

there are chimneys under the sea. *Black smokers are formed when hot springs on the seabed gush out water that is black with metals.* The metals harden in the cold water, forming tall chimneys.

The world's longest mountain range is the Mid-Oceanic Ridge, a string of volcanoes underwater. Submersibles such as *Alvin* go down and photograph it.

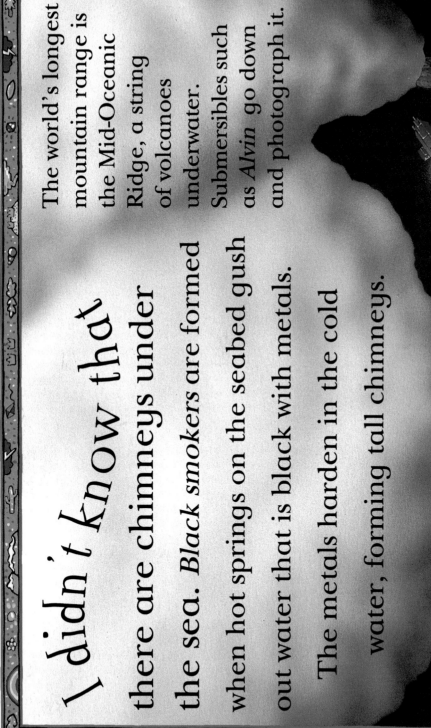

Alvin

20

True or false?
There are pillows on the seabed.

Answer: **True**
Underwater volcanoes erupt slowly because of the weight of the water. Their lava cools to form lumps called pillows.

The black smokers leak out poisonous sulfur. Even so, giant tube worms (left) live in the pitch-black water around them, feeding on the sulfur-rich bacteria there.

Swarms of shrimp feed around the chimneys on the bacteria in the water. Spots on their backs can detect the glow given out by the black smokers.

Most of the earth's volcanoes are under the sea.

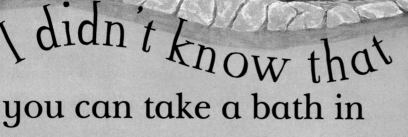

I didn't know that

you can take a bath in mud. Volcanic heat underground can cause hot springs and bubbling mud pools. Though some pools are boiling hot and would scald your skin, others are cool enough to bathe in. People wallow in the warm mud. The minerals in the mud leave skin feeling soft and smooth.

The Japanese town of Beppu has 4,000 hot springs all to itself. The Jungle Bath (above), at over 64,000 sq ft, is the biggest spa in the world.

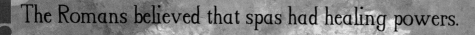
The Romans believed that spas had healing powers.

Steam power from hot springs can be used to make electricity.

True or false?
Volcanoes have healing powers.

Answer: **True**
It can't be proven for sure, but lots of people believe they do! In Japan, people like to get up to their necks in warm volcanic sand (left). They believe it can cure illnesses. Drinking the mineral-rich water from hot springs is thought to keep the body healthy and bathing in hot springs soothes pain.

SEARCH & FIND
Can you find the swimming cap?
FIND & SEARCH

I didn't know that

volcanoes fall asleep for centuries. Between eruptions, volcanoes sleep, or are *dormant*. In the Auvergne region of France are remains of *extinct* volcanoes. The *cone* is weathered away but the hard vent is left. It is hard to be sure that a volcano is really extinct.

True or false?
Volcanoes make money.

Answer: **True**
They provide us with precious and useful minerals that formed millions of years ago in the hardening lava. This South African diamond mine (right) at Kimberley is on the site of an extinct volcano.

Nogorongoro, an extinct volcano in Tanzania (right), is home to flamingos and hippos. Its crater is a lake and the lush grassland around it feeds rhinos and zebras.

Two volcanoes that erupted in Turkey eight million years ago have long disappeared. But the lava left behind a "city" of fairytale cones, into which people dug houses and churches that can still be seen today.

Volcano remains at Le Puy, France

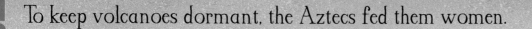

To keep volcanoes dormant, the Aztecs fed them women.

True or false?

The largest volcano is in space.

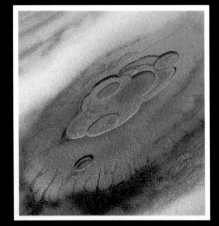

I didn't know that

there are volcanoes in space. One of Jupiter's moons, Io, is covered in erupting volcanoes. The two *Voyager* spacecraft sent back photographs of the volcanic gas clouds there – which were higher than 30 Mount Everests!

Answer: **True**
The largest known volcano isn't on Earth at all! Mars is home to Olympus Mons, which is 300 miles across and 16 miles high. Like all Mars' volcanoes, Olympus Mons is extinct.

Closer to home, there are volcanoes on our moon, and on Mars and Venus. The *Magellan* spacecraft used radar to take pictures of Venus' volcanoes.

Most craters we see on planets are from meteorites, not volcanoes.

Voyager

27

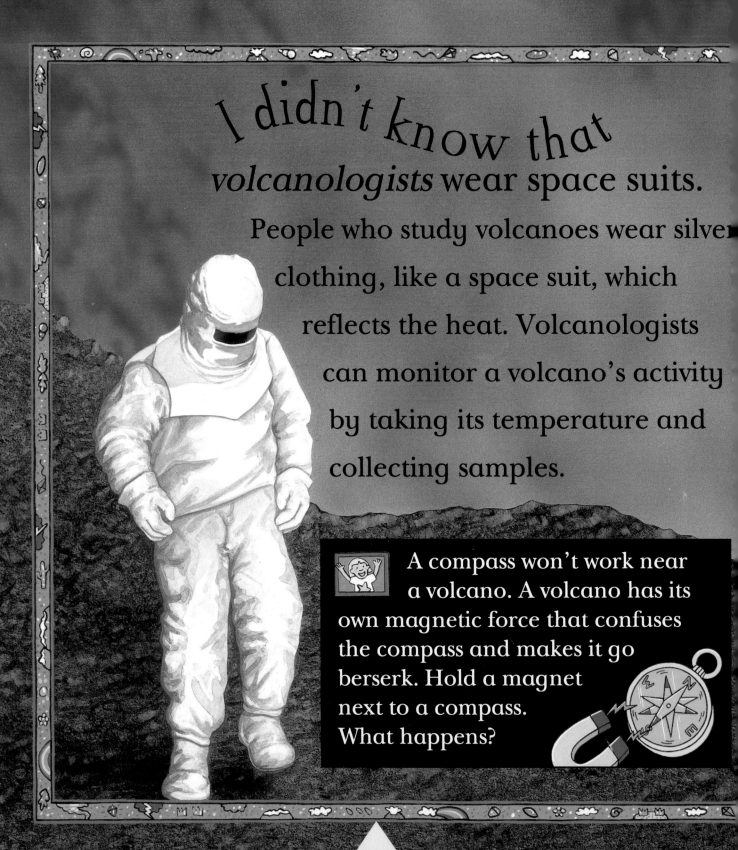

I didn't know that

volcanologists wear space suits.

People who study volcanoes wear silver clothing, like a space suit, which reflects the heat. Volcanologists can monitor a volcano's activity by taking its temperature and collecting samples.

A compass won't work near a volcano. A volcano has its own magnetic force that confuses the compass and makes it go berserk. Hold a magnet next to a compass. What happens?

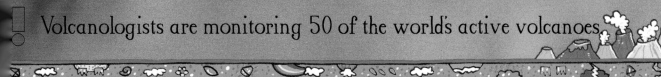

In areas where there are lots of volcanoes, people have to prepare for emergencies. This is a lava bomb shelter in Sakurajima, Japan. Inside, people are safe from the showers of lava bombs.

Volcanologists take samples of lava to examine in the laboratory. They swirl a long pole into the flow to collect it – just like cotton candy collects around its wooden stick.

Volcanologists wear gas masks so they don't breathe in poisonous gases, or choke on ash. Finding out about volcanoes is a dangerous job. When volcanologists can forecast eruptions, they can save lives.

Glossary

Black smoker
A hot spring on the ocean floor.

Caldera
A huge volcanic crater, formed when the slopes of a volcano collapse into the empty magma chamber.

Cone
The "mountain" of hardened lava that builds up around a volcano.

Core
The center of the earth.

Crater
The bowl-shaped hollow at the top of a volcano, above the vent.

Crust
The outer layer of the earth.

Dormant
A volcano is dormant, or sleeping, between eruptions.

Eruption
The way a volcano throws out gases, rocks, and ash onto the earth's surface.

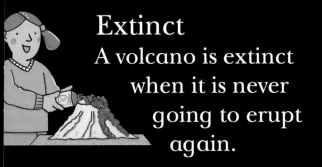

Extinct
A volcano is extinct when it is never going to erupt again.

Fault lines
Cracks in the earth's crust.

Geyser
A fountain of water heated by volcanic activity underground.

Lava
Magma that has reached the earth's surface. It cools as flows on land or pillows under the sea.

Magma
Hot molten rock that is still below the earth's surface.

Mantle
The hot layer of the earth between the crust and the core.

Plates
Large sections of the earth's crust that are constantly moving against each other.

Tsunami
A giant wave, caused by a volcanic eruption or an earthquake.

Volcanologist
Someone who studies volcanoes.

Index

Alvin 20
ash 12, 13, 14, 15, 29
Aztecs 25

black smokers 20, 21, 30

caldera 9, 30
chimneys 20, 21
cone 8, 24, 25, 30
core 9, 30, 31
crater 8, 9, 24, 26, 30
creepmeter 7

diamonds 24
dormant volcanoes 24, 25, 28, 30

earthquakes 6, 7, 16
earth's crust 7, 8, 9, 30, 31
Easter Island 16
electricity 12, 23
extinct volcanoes 24, 25, 26, 31

fault lines 6, 7, 31

geysers 8, 18, 31

hot springs 20, 22, 23, 30

Iceland 13, 18, 19

Jupiter 26

Krakatoa 16

lapilli 10
lava 10, 11, 24, 25, 29, 30, 31
lava bombs 10, 11, 29
lava pillows 21, 31
lightning 12

magma 8, 9, 30, 31
magnetism 28
mantle 9, 31
meteorites 26
Mid-Oceanic Ridge 18, 20
moon 12, 26
Mount Fujiyama 17
Mount St. Helens 12, 13
Mount Vesuvius 14

mud pools 22

Olympus Mons 26

pahoehoe 11
pipe 8
plates 6, 7, 31
Pliny the Elder 14
Pompeii 14, 15
pumice stone 10

Ring of Fire 6
Romans 14, 15, 22

San Andreas Fault 7
sulfur 21
Surtsey 18, 19

tsunami 16, 17, 31

vent 24
Venus 26, 27
volcanologists 28, 29, 31
Voyager 26, 27
Vulcan 8

Titles available in the series:
I Didn't Know That

The **sun** is a star
You can jump higher on the **moon**
Some **snakes** spit poison
Some **bugs** glow in the dark
Spiders have fangs
Some **birds** hang upside down
Dinosaurs laid eggs
Some **trains** run on water
Some **planes** hover
Some **plants** grow in midair
Sharks keep losing their teeth
People chase **twisters**
Mountains gush lava and ash
Chimps use tools
Some **boats** have wings
Whales can sing
Only some **big cats** can roar
Crocodiles yawn to keep cool